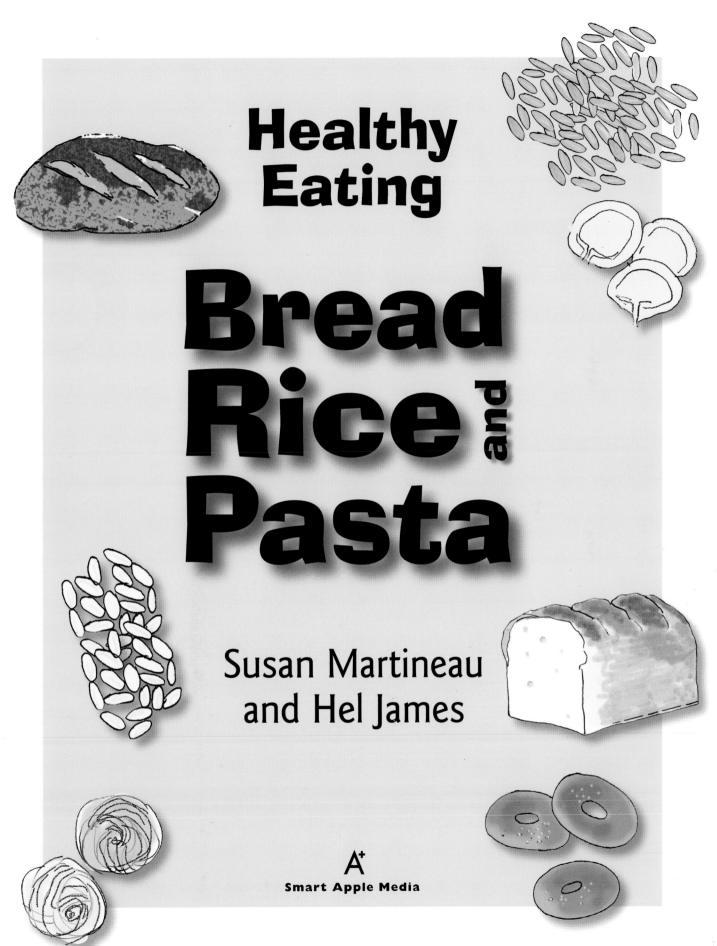

Healthy Eating

Bread Rice and Pasta

Susan Martineau and Hel James

A+

Smart Apple Media

Published by Smart Apple Media
2140 Howard Drive West, North Mankato, MN 56003

Designed and illustrated by Helen James
Edited by Jinny Johnson

Photographs: 10-11 James Marshall/Corbis; 12-13 Susan Martineau; 16 PhotoCuisine/Corbis; 18-19 Tom
Bean/Corbis; 21 Charles Gupton/Corbis; 25 Vittoriano Rastelli/Corbis; 29 Michael Freeman/Corbis
Front cover: James Noble/Corbis

Printed in Thailand

Library of Congress Catalog-in-Publication Data

Martineau, Susan.
Healthy eating. Bread, rice, and pasta / by Susan Martineau.
p. cm.
Includes index.
ISBN-13: 978-1-58340-894-0
1. Bread—Juvenile literature. 2. Rice—Juvenile literature. 3. Pasta products—Juvenile literature. I. Title. II.
Title: Bread, rice, and pasta.

TX769.M335 2006
641.3'03—dc22   2006008870

First Edition
9 8 7 6 5 4 3 2 1

Contents

Food for health

Our bodies are like amazing machines.
Just like machines, we need the right
kind of fuel to give us energy and
to keep us working properly.

If we don't eat the kind of food we need to keep us healthy, we may become ill or feel tired and grumpy. Our bodies do not like it if we eat too much of one kind of food, such as cakes or chips.

We need a balanced diet. That means eating different kinds of good food in the right amounts.

You'll be surprised at how much there is to know about where our food comes from and why some kinds of food are better for us than others. Finding out about food is great fun and very tasty!

I'm really hungry.

A balanced meal!

The good things, or **nutrients**, that our bodies need come from different kinds of food. Let's look at what your plate should have on it. It all looks delicious!

Rice, bread, and pasta

These foods contain **carbohydrates**, and they give us energy. They are also called starchy foods. About a third of your food should come from this group.

Fruits and vegetables

Rice, bread, and pasta

Chicken with rice and vegetables makes a great balanced meal.

Fruits and vegetables

These are full of great **vitamins**, **minerals**, and **fiber**. They do all kinds of useful jobs in your body to help keep you healthy. About a third of our food should come from this group.

Meat, fish, and eggs

Protein from these helps your body grow and repair itself. They are body-building foods. We should eat some of them every day.

Milk, yogurt, and cheese

These **dairy foods** give us protein and **calcium** to make strong bones and teeth.

Sugar and fats

Eat only small amounts of these. Too much can be bad for our teeth and make us overweight.

Milk, yogurt, and cheese

Sugar and fats

Meat, fish, and eggs

Water

We need to drink at least six glasses of water every day.

Energy foods

Try to eat a portion of energy food at every meal. Make a super-charged menu for the day with lots of energy foods.

Super-charged menu

Breakfast

A big bowl of cereal with fruit or a bowl of oatmeal makes a very good breakfast.

Rice, bread, and pasta are our main power-packed foods. Some other foods, such as breakfast cereals and potatoes, give us energy too.

Breakfast is a great start to the day.

Super-charged menu

Lunch

Enjoy a sandwich or roll with your favorite filling.

Did you know you use energy even when you're sitting down?

Super-charged menu

Dinner

Eat a dish of pasta, noodles, or rice with tasty vegetables or meat.

A bowl of rice

Rice grains are the seeds of the rice plant. It is a **cereal plant**, like wheat, oats, or barley.

Rice grows in many parts of the world, but most comes from Asia, America, and Australia. The rice plants grow best when their roots are under water. That is why rice fields, or paddy fields, are very wet places.

In Asia, the rice plants are planted in the fields by hand. In America and Australia, the rice seeds are dropped by an airplane.

Ancient food

In Asia, rice has been grown and eaten for 5,000 years. In places like China and India, people often eat rice two or three times a day.

Harvesting rice

When the rice has grown and is ready to be **harvested**, it is cut by hand or by huge machines called combines. The rice grains then have to be separated from the stalks.

Brown rice

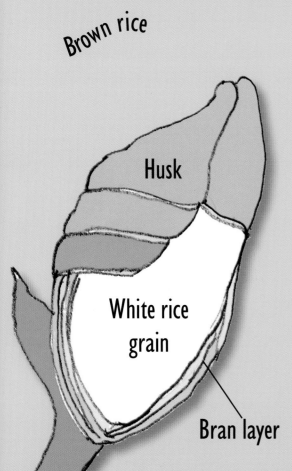

Husk

White rice grain

Bran layer

Hard husks on the outside of the grain are taken off to make the rice ready for us to eat. This leaves a layer of **bran** on the grain and gives us brown rice. Bran is very good for you because it contains vitamins and fiber.

This bran layer is usually removed to make the white rice we see in stores. White rice is still a very good energy food, but brown rice is better for us.

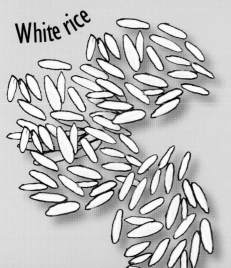

White rice

In Asia, the grains and stalks are separated by hand. In America and Australia, this is done by machines.

13

Know your rice!

Rice is used in many delicious dishes around the world. It can be eaten hot or cold, in sweet or salty foods. There are three main types of rice: long-grain, medium-grain, and short-grain.

Basmati is a long-grain rice used in Indian cookery. The grains do not stick together when they are cooked. Basmati is great with curries.

Arborio is a medium-grain rice. It is used in a tasty Italian dish called risotto.

Try cooking some rice yourself, but ask an adult to help.

Short-grain rice becomes sticky when it is cooked, so it's good for rice pudding.

Rice spotter

Next time you are in a food store or supermarket, see how many types of rice you can find. Which ones have you tried eating?

Breakfast boost

Rice grains are made into breakfast food by puffing them up. Other grains from cereal plants, such as oats, barley, and wheat, are also used to make breakfast cereals. Corn flakes are made from corn. Extra vitamins, minerals, and **iron** are added to breakfast cereals to make them even better for you.

Cereal, milk, and fruit make a nutrient-packed start to your day.

The best breakfast cereals are the ones made with whole grains or wheat. Look for the words "**whole grain**" or "**whole wheat**" on the cereal box.

Sugar alert

Some breakfast cereals have a lot of sugar. Look at the list of ingredients. If sugar is near the top of the list, choose another kind of cereal. Too much sugar is bad for your teeth!

Try this one!

Too much sugar!

Bring on the bread

Bread is made from flour and water. Flour is made by grinding up the grains from cereal plants. Most of the bread we eat is made from wheat flour. Flour can also be made from corn, rye, or oats.

White, or refined, flour is made from grinding only the inside of the grains of wheat. To make whole wheat or whole grain flour, whole grains are ground, including the skin, or bran. This flour is better for us because it contains more vitamins, minerals, and fiber.

The grain is harvested using massive machines called combines.

Wheat grain

Inside of the grain

Bran

Making bread

Some people make their own bread at home, but most of us buy bread from a bakery or supermarket. This bread is made in **factory bakeries** by huge machines.

Flour, water, salt, and **yeast** are measured into enormous tubs and mixed together to make **dough**. The dough is cut into pieces and put into tins. It is left alone while the yeast makes it "rise" or get bigger. Then it is put into a giant oven to be baked.

Some of the loaves are kept whole and some are sliced before being put into packaging and sent to stores.

Mix flour, water, and yeast to make dough.

Knead the dough, then put it in a bowl and leave it to rise.

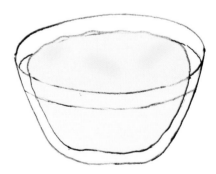

Eat it up!

Bread doesn't keep for very long and is best eaten when it is fresh. Dates on labels tell you how soon the bread should be eaten.

Put the dough in a pan.

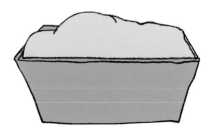

Bake it in the oven.

A world of bread

There are so many delicious breads to try. Next time you go shopping, look at some different types and choose a new one to try. Bread can be eaten with all kinds of meals.

This one's whole wheat!

Whole wheat loaves and rolls

These are really good for you, but check the labels for the words "whole wheat" or "whole grain." Then you know it's the best of brown bread!

Ciabatta, bagels, and baguettes

These are made with white or refined flour. They still add energy to your lunchbox, but whole wheat bread is better for you.

Add your own filling to a pita.

Chapatis, pita breads, and tortillas

These are **unleavened** or flat breads made without yeast. They can be used for scooping or wrapping food.

23

Oodles of noodles

Pasta and noodles are another energy-packed food that is eaten all over the world. Italian-style pasta is made from wheat flour and water. Pasta, like bread, can be made with whole wheat or white flour. Sometimes egg or oil is added, too. Tomato or spinach can also be added for extra color and flavor.

Fresh or dried?

You can buy fresh or dried pasta. Fresh pasta does not keep for long. Dried pasta can keep for up to two years!

SNAP!

Fresh pasta is soft and floppy; dried pasta is hard and brittle.

**The dried pasta shapes you see
in stores are made in factories.**

In the pasta factories, flour and water are
made into dough in huge tubs. Then the
dough is shaped to make different types of
pasta, dried, and put into bags or packages.

Piles of pasta

Did you know that there are more than 600 different pasta shapes? You won't find all of them in your local supermarket, but you could have some fun seeing how many kinds you can spot.

Pasta provides us with carbohydrates. When it is served with some meat or vegetable sauce, it makes the kind of balanced meal that our bodies like.

Tasty parcels

These tubes, or packages, of pasta contain tasty mixtures of meat, cheese, and vegetables.

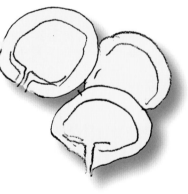

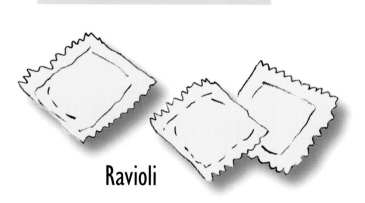

Ravioli

Tortelloni

Cannelloni

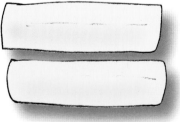

Fun shapes

Even the names of these are fun.

Penne — quills

Farfalle — butterflies
or bow-ties

Fusilli — spirals

Conchiglie — shells

Long and thin

Eat these with your favorite meat or
vegetable sauce or just sprinkle
some cheese on top.

Linguine

Tagliatelle

Spaghetti

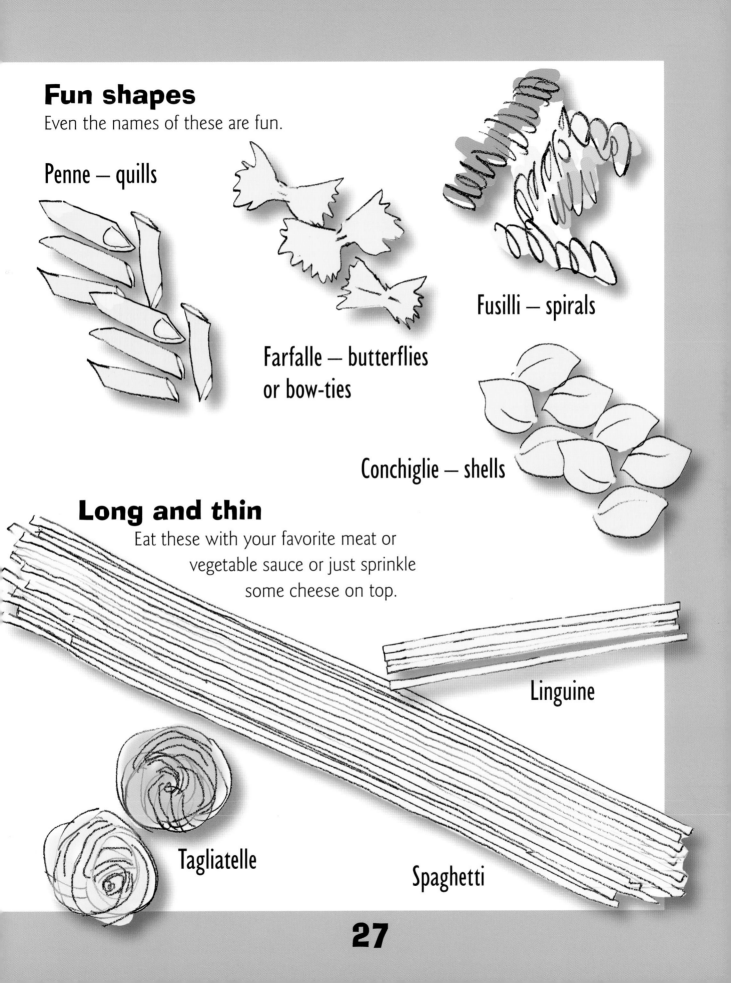

Oriental noodles

Asian-style noodles are also made from wheat flour and water. Sometimes egg is added to make delicious yellow egg noodles. Noodles can be made with other types of flour too. Rice noodles are made from rice flour and cellophane noodles from ground-up mung beans.

SLURP!

In Asia, you can buy these noodles all freshly made. In other places, you can buy them dried in packets. They can all be made into great **nutritious** meals.

Noodle soups and stir-fries are healthy meals. Choose your favorite vegetables, fish, or meat and add them to noodle soup or stir-fried noodles. Then slurp them up!

How
many
different
kinds of
noodles
can you
see?

Words to remember

bran   The thin, brown layer underneath the husks of cereal grains. Bran contains iron and B vitamins.

calcium   A mineral that helps build healthy bones and teeth. Dairy foods are high in calcium.

carbohydrates   The starches and sugars in food that give us energy. Rice, pasta, bread, and potatoes are all carbohydrate foods.

cereal plants   These are types of grass plants grown for food. Examples are wheat, rice, rye, corn, barley, and oats.

dairy foods   Foods made from milk, such as cheese, butter, cream, and yogurt.

dough   A soft, thick mixture made of flour and water.

factory bakeries   A place where bread is made in very large quantities to supply supermarkets and stores.

fiber   This is found in plant foods, such as grains and vegetables. It helps our insides work properly.

harvested   When crops are cut down and gathered for food.

iron   A mineral found in food that we need to keep our blood healthy.

minerals   Nutrients in food that help our bodies work properly. Calcium and iron are minerals.

nutrients   Parts of food that your body needs to make energy, to grow healthily, and to repair itself.

nutritious   Containing lots of nutrients.

protein   Body-building food that makes our bodies grow well and stay healthy.

whole grain or whole wheat   Bread and cereals made using the whole grains of cereal plants like wheat.

unleavened   Bread made without using yeast to make it rise.

vitamins   Nutrients in food which help our bodies work properly. The B vitamins in bran help to turn our food into energy and also help our muscles, skin, and blood.

yeast   Yeast is added to dough to make it puff up and make bread with bubbles in it.

Index

Web sites

Learn which foods make a healthy heart.
http://www.healthyfridge.org/

Test your nutritional knowledge with quizzes, dietary guidelines, and a glossary of terms.
http://www.exhibits.pacsci.org/nutrition/

Find out how to have a healthy diet without eating meat.
http://www.vrg.org/family/kidsindex.htm

Get the facts about fast food restaurants and tips for making healthy choices.
http://library.thinkquest.org/4485/

Take the 5-a-day challenge and learn about fruits and vegetables with puzzles, music, and games.
http://www.dole5aday.com/

Discover ten tips for a healthy lifestyle.
http://www.fitness.gov/l0tips.htm